Gallery Books
Editor: Peter Fallon

CATCHPENNY TWIST

Stewart Parker

Catchpenny Twist

 Gallery Books

Catchpenny Twist
is first published
simultaneously in
paperback and in a
clothbound edition
in 1980.

The Gallery Press
19 Oakdown Road
Dublin 14
Ireland.

Cover design by Michael Kane

ISBN 0 904011 12 7 (cloth)
        904011 13 5 (paper)

The Gallery Press gratefully acknowledges the assistance of The
Arts Council of Northern Ireland towards the publication of this
book.

Catchpenny Twist

A charade in two acts

Catchpenny Twist was first performed in the Peacock Theatre, Dublin, on Thursday, 25 August 1977 with the following cast:

Martyn Semple	Desmond Cave
Roy Fletcher	Raymond Hardie
Monagh Cahoon	Deirdre Donnelly
Marie Kyle	Ingrid Craigie
The Man	Des Keogh
The Woman	Billie Morton
The Girl	Fiona MacAnna

The musicians were Jolyon Jackson, Greg Boland, Garvan Gallagher, Fran Breen and Paul McAteer.

Direction	Patrick Laffan
Settings and Costumes	Wendy Shea
Lighting	Tony Wakefield
Sound	Brian Collins

for Kate

Characters

Roy Fletcher
Martyn Semple
Monagh Cahoon
Marie Kyle
The Vocal Trio—Man, Woman, Girl
                 —who between them play all the
                 other parts

Four Piece Band: lead and bass guitars,
                 keyboards, drums/percussion.

ACT ONE

SCHOOL HALL

> *Music.* ROY, MARTYN *and* MONAGH *stride on in a follow spot, holding each others' waists, dressed in gowns and mortar-boards.*

Song   Pack up your bags, pack up your books,
Get off to where the sunshine really cooks
The dream boat's leaving
The magic carpet's weaving
Over the Assembly Hall,
Round the boundary wall,

Pick up your fags, pick up your feet,
We'll soon be on our way to Easy Street,
The steamboat's puffing
The gravy train is chuffing
So go wherever Destiny awaits thee —
And you can't go soon enough
No you can't go soon enough
You can't go soon enough for me!

> *They take a bow. The* MAN—*as a Headmaster—sweeps on, arm extended towards them.*

MAN   Our fiddlers three, the masters and mistress of terpsichore and rhyme, give them a bit of a hand now! *(He leads the clapping).* Come on, show grateful, hands out of pockets for once in the year! *(Gestures abruptly for applause to cease).* It's in that proper spirit of appreciation and indeed gratitude for where would we be in these dark days of strife without an occasional quip and a jolly snatch of song on our lips to lift the heart and quicken the step . . . that's the spirit as I say in which as always on these end of term occasions of frolic that I extend an emphatic thank-you in all our behalf from the whole school, to Miss Cahoon, Mr. Semple and Mr. Fletcher, for their mirthful mouthfuls and their witty ditties! Now it only remains for me to wish you all a happy holiday— an industrious holiday—and above all a well-conducted holiday, for I don't want to be reading any of your names in the headlines this summer, I have no wish to

11

see the good name of the school being dragged through the courts of law yet again and especially not in connection with guns and explosives! Right. Dismiss.

Blackout.

CLASSROOM

> *Raucous laughter from* MONAGH *and* MARTYN *is heard in the darkness. They are seen, as the fluorescent lighting flickers on, removing their gowns and mortarboards.* ROY *is opening a bottle of champagne.*

ROY   It didn't turn out the way I thought it would.

MONAGH   No post-mortems, please, we got through it.

ROY   Fell through it, more like.

MARTYN   You could sing that, you know. If you had a tune to it. Falling Through . . . a song for horny window-cleaners.

> ROY *pops the cork and pours the champagne into glasses.*

MONAGH   A fine young sparkling cider, I suppose?

ROY   Do you mind—it's the genuine article.

MARTYN   'The true, the blushful Hippocrene, winking at the brim'.

ROY   You both owe me for it.

MONAGH   *(to* MARTYN*)* So young and yet so profligate!

ROY   It's scandalously over-priced.

MARTYN   What the hell—Happy Anniversary. *(He drinks).*

MONAGH   Mud in your eye. *(Drinks).*

ROY   Absent friend. *(Drinks).*

MONAGH   Thanks, that's real cheery. Enter the ghost at the banquet. *(to* MARTYN*)* Have you seen her recently?

MARTYN   She's been up in court. Possession of a dangerous weapon. With intent to endanger life. Why do they say that? You would hardly have it to hammer in nails with.

MONAGH   You've got to hand it to Marie Kyle, raving mad as she is. At least she has the courage of her convictions.

MARTYN   She hasn't had a conviction yet, the judge let her go.

ROY   *(to* MARTYN*)* You're a tonic, you know that?

MONAGH   All we ever shoot off is our mouths.

ROY   We?

MONAGH   Yes, We . . . you and him and me. We're still here, aren't we? After seven years? Still stuck in the same hole? Enjoying our seventh annual end-of-term frolic? Christ, just look at this school. It's a clapped-out shell. It's a jerry-built seven-year-old ruin. You could punch your way out through the walls.

MARTYN   Most of the third-year kids already have.

MONAGH   Right, they're out in the streets fighting a war, and what am I doing? Teaching the rest of them to sing 'The Skye Boat Song'.

ROY   I know what you're saying, it's age. I saw a girl in the playground this afternoon. She wasn't in her school uniform. She was in a suede skirt. Talk about lubricious . . . I'd never clapped eyes on the like of it. And then I suddenly realised—it wasn't a girl at all. It was a girl's mother. *(He reflects)*. I never would have believed that it would come to that. Fancying the mothers.

MONAGH   Is this the best you can manage? Middle-aged lechery?

ROY   We should have done the strip number.

MONAGH   Oh certainly—with me flying kamikaze and you two on the ground crew.

ROY   By God that would have put ould Cochrane's nose out of joint, all the same.

MARTYN   More than his nose. *(Imitating the Headmaster)*. Come on come on hands out of pockets for once in the year! *(He has a hand thrust in his trouser pocket to suggest an erection)*.

MONAGH   You've been repeating this every year for seven years now. My God, think of it. Seven of them. Think of what's been happening to this country. It's clean passed us by. We're not even relevant.

ROY   Who needs it? All I want is out.

MARTYN   None of us ever intended to be teachers, remember?

MONAGH   I can't even say I've been unhappy. There's nothing as definite as that. Whenever I think it over, when I weigh it up moment by moment—it all seems as good as you can expect. But if I look back on a week or a month—it always turns out to be as bad as you can get. Like as if the best you can say about anything is—it could be worse. It could be worse. What kind of an epitaph is that?

MARTYN   'It could have *been* worse'.

MONAGH   What?

MARTYN   For an epitaph you would need to say 'It could have *been* worse'.

MONAGH	Wanker!
ROY	Take it easy.
MONAGH	I'm trying to express despair and he gives me English grammar!
ROY	This summer—Fletcher and Semple make the big break.
MONAGH	. . . and only at the seventh attempt, listeners.
ROY	We've got experience behind us now. Three songs in professional circulation.
MONAGH	Don't forget to call in and show me your Oscar.
ROY	At least we've got plans. What are your plans?
MONAGH	I'm still making plans for my twenty-first birthday party. You might not remember, but I came down with shingles two days before it.
MARTYN	I remember that. I sent you Polaroid photographs of Marie and me singing Happy Birthday.
MONAGH	I still haven't decided what to wear. Perhaps the Lurex halter top and the green silk harem pants . . . set off by a polished emerald in the navel . . .

ROY *begins to vocalise some strip-tease music, clapping his hands.* MARTYN *joins in.* MONAGH *goes into a half-parodied strip routine. As the tempo increases, the drums join in.* MARTYN *and* ROY *are on their knees. When* MONAGH *is down to her underclothes, the headmaster suddenly enters wearing an appalled expression. They freeze. Silence.*
Blackout.

STREET

MARIE KYLE *and the* WOMAN, *in raincoats, are standing studying a copy of the Irish News.*

MARIE	There you are. Deaths. Three columns all to himself. It's a credit to you to have borne a son like that.
WOMAN	It would have made him very proud. He was a good Catholic boy and never did a wrong thing to nobody.
MARIE	He died a patriot's death and it'll never be forgotten.
WOMAN	God bless you, Marie. I'll take this home and clip it out to keep.

14

MARTYN *has appeared, walking towards them, holding up an open umbrella.*

MARTYN Hello, Marie.
WOMAN   I'm away, love, I'll be seeing you.
MARIE   Yes indeed, bye-bye.

The WOMAN *goes off.*

        What are you doing out of school at this hour?
MARTYN I got the sack.
MARIE   You never did.
MARTYN Roy and Monagh as well. All three of us. We were just horsing around after the end-of-term revue. When in walks Cochrane. And that was it. Curtains.
MARIE   You were never that serious about teaching, were you?
MARTYN It was a job.
MARIE   You were never too serious about anything.
MARTYN One or two things, Marie. You and the night and the music.

        The MAN *and* GIRL, *as a military police patrol, have appeared and are approaching them.*

MARIE   Kiss me.
MARTYN What?

        She pulls his free arm round her shoulders, embraces him tightly and kisses him. The MAN *and* GIRL *pass by them, smiling, the* MAN *whistling softly at them, and stroll off.*

MARIE   *(disengaging abruptly)* Sorry about that.
MARTYN Don't be sorry.
MARIE   Those English bastards have photographs of me now.
MARTYN Is that why you've dyed your hair?
MARIE   It's easier if you're a man, you can grow a beard.
MARTYN It looks nice that way.
        (Slight pause)
MARIE   What will you do now?
MARTYN We're living on the dole. Trying to write songs.
MARIE   Any luck?
MARTYN In this town? You're joking.

15

MARIE	I might be able to put some work your way.
MARTYN	You?
MARIE	Ever try writing ballads?
MARTYN	You mean street ballads? Come-all-ye's? Sure they're traditional, nobody writes those.
MARIE	Traditions need to be maintained. *(She starts to walk off)*. It's worth thirty pounds a throw, if you're interested at all.
MARTYN	Tell me more.

He follows her. They go off together.
Music.

STAGE

A spot appears on the WOMAN *standing at a microphone as a folk-singer, in a mantilla and green peasant-style dress. Behind her is a large Sacred Heart portrait of Jesus.*

WOMAN *(sings)* He came forth in some poor hovel
With the livestock close at hand
But his mother smiled upon him
He was born for Ireland

In his father's holy temple
He was forced to make a stand
He drove out the money-changers
For the sake of Ireland

Forty days he was forsaken
Foul temptation did withstand
Then to the foe he was delivered
By a traitor's cruel hand

So he died in brave defiance
Crucified by their command
But on Easter Monday morning
He rose again for Ireland.

Blackout.

16

MARTYN is seated at a typewriter. ROY is standing about aimlessly.

MARTYN   What's another word for 'nation'?

ROY   Country.

MARTYN   No good.

ROY   Land.

MARTYN   Longer.

ROY   Mausoleum.
(Pause)
Look at the time.

MARTYN   Don't fluster me.

ROY   Is that her?

They listen intently for a moment. Silence.

MARTYN   I do the words, you stick to the music.

ROY   What music? They're only after the usual traditional whinge.

MARTYN   'Then sing with me this ballad Of the death of Sean McVeigh, He will not be forgotten' . . . Not for a day or two, anyway.

ROY   Are you looking shot?

MARTYN   She's lost her sense of humour, Marie. *(Pause)*. What rhymes with McVeigh?

ROY   Slay.

MARTYN   Pray? . . . Obey?

ROY   Decay.

MARTYN   Great. Thanks. That's terrific. 'He gave his life for Ireland, On account of tooth decay'.

ROY   She'll be here any minute, you know.

MARTYN   We were mad to take this on, Roy.

ROY   It's work. It's money.

MARTYN   It's not real. I'm a pacifist.

ROY   Fine, if you want to hunt for another teaching job, go ahead.

MARTYN   What's the use? You can imagine asking Cochrane for a reference. *(Imitating)*. 'Pure filth'. He really had us nailed to the wall. Lewd and indecent behaviour in the very classroom.

ROY   My only regret is, it didn't happen sooner.

MARTYN   The drink he might have overlooked—what with being

	an alcoholic—but Monagh in her undies, that was the three of us blacklisted for keeps.
ROY	Listen, you know as well as I do—those schools are just child labour camps. You're not hired as a teacher at all, you're hired as a commandant.
MARTYN	He was beside himself with glee, of course, the old fart. He'd been waiting seven years for a chance like that.
ROY	It was our good luck, not his. We were in the wrong business, Sempo. At least we're on our way now.
	(Slight pause)
MARTYN	What about Monagh?
ROY	Have you heard anything?
MARTYN	Not since she went down to Dublin.
ROY	She's a bit old to start a singing career.
MARTYN	Aren't we all.
ROY	Although she could pass for twenty-five.
MARTYN	On a good night. If the lighting was right.
	(Slight pause)
	What happened to her distinguished lover in television?
ROY	Still plugged in, as far as I hear.
MARTYN	Playfair . . . it's an odd name.
ROY	Doesn't quite suit in his case, he's married with four brats.
MARTYN	It rhymes with Mayfair, though.
ROY	So?
MARTYN	McVeigh . . . McVeigh . . .
ROY	What about 'array' . . . 'affray' . . . 'say nay' . . .
MARTYN	What do you think this is, Alexander Pope?
ROY	What about 'weigh' . . . *(he mimes scales)* . . . or 'way' *(he indicates direction)* . . .
MARTYN	Wait a minute, it's coming *(he starts scribbling)*.
ROY	'Old and grey'.
MARTYN	Shut up. I'm getting it.

The doorbell rings.

	Don't answer it. *(He gets up)*. You type. (ROY *sits at the typewriter)*. Are you ready?
ROY	Chrissake get on with it!
MARTYN	*(dictating)* 'A British soldier cursed at him' . . . (ROY *types)* . . . 'A British soldier cursed at him' . . . 'As his life-blood flowed away', no, 'ebbed away' . . .

The doorbell rings.

ROY   We'll have to let her in.
MARTYN   . . . 'as his life-blood ebbed away' . . . (ROY *types*) . . .
           'But Ireland's sons will not forget' . . .
ROY   Will not what?
MARTYN   Will not forget, 'But Ireland's sons will not forget' . . .
           (ROY *types; the door is knocked*) . . . 'the name of Sean
           McVeigh'. Read it over.
ROY   (*reading it*) A British soldier cursed at him As his life-
           blood ebbed away But Ireland's sons will not forget
           The name of Sean McVeigh.
MARTYN   Not bad, sure it isn't?
ROY   Open the bloody door!

> MARTYN *rushes out to hall door.* ROY *staples the lyric*
> *sheet to the music hastily, then crams it into an envelope.*
> MARTYN *returns with* MARIE.

MARTYN   (*re-entering*) How are things with you, Marie?
MARIE   I was just on the point of giving up.
MARTYN   We were putting the bins out.
ROY   Here's the stuff.
           (*He hands her the envelope. She takes the song out and*
           starts to read it).
MARTYN   I'll put the kettle on.
MARIE   Not for me.
MARTYN   You've time for a coffee.
MARIE   They're waiting for this, down in the studio.
ROY   You people certainly work fast.
MARIE   It's urgent business we're on. (*She pockets the song*).
           That's quite satisfactory. (*She pulls out three crumpled*
           ten pound notes and throws them carelessly on to the
           desk).
ROY   Is that your thirty-pieces-of-silver gesture?
MARIE   (*to* MARTYN) We lost a volunteer called Quigley last
           night.
MARTYN   Yeah, the van driver, I heard it on the news. (*Slight*
           pause). You want a ballad.
MARIE   I'll call on Friday. Right?
MARIE   (*glancing at* ROY) Friday. Sure. Okay.
MARIE   Here's the clipping about it. (*She gives him a newspaper*
           cutting). His widow has specially requested 'Four Green
           Fields' as the air.
MARTYN   Fine. Right. So. How've you been keeping, Marie?
MARIE   My health's excellent, thank you.

ROY	How's the tightness round your arse?
MARIE	*(going)* See you.
ROY	Shot anyone interesting lately?
MARTYN	*(to* MARIE*)* He hasn't changed, same old joker. *(To* ROY*)* Easy on.
ROY	She's not going to walk in here and act as if we were some unpleasant form of plant life!
MARIE	*(going)* You can sort this out between you.
ROY	We want no part of your doings.
MARIE	*(holding up the envelope)* What do you call this?
ROY	Gunk.
MARIE	*(pointing to the money)* I have a similar name for that.

She goes. MARTYN *follows.*

MARTYN	Friday at the same time then, Marie.

ROY, *left alone, thumps the furniture. The door is heard closing, off.* MARTYN *re-enters.*

ROY	The smug stuck-up piece of scrag!
MARTYN	*(sniffing)* Smell that perfume?
ROY	Typical Irish bitch . . .
MARTYN	Odour of sanctity, it's called.
ROY	You couldn't prise her knees apart with one of her own bombs. *(He follows her off)*. I hope the Special Branch gets you!
MARTYN	*(looking at clipping)* What rhymes with 'Quigley'?
ROY	*(re-entering)* Here, we've got some letters. *(He's been opening one)*. Look at this—from the agency. *(Reads it)*. They're offering us a jingle.
MARTYN	Seriously?
ROY	Yeah.
MARTYN	Sensational! What's it for?
ROY	Brady's Frozen Chickens.
MARTYN	That's great. *(He considers)*. Putting the freeze on . . . there's a lot of possibilities . . . getting the bird!
ROY	We're on our way.
MARTYN	If this one hits, it'll break us into the market!
ROY	Make your mark with commercials and you're a gilt-edged songwriter, no looking back.
MARTYN	It's a real opening.
ROY	We're going to make it big, Sempo. Stick with your Uncle Roy.

20

He's been opening the other letter. He shakes two objects out of it into his hand.

MARTYN   What's that?
ROY   Two bullets.

Blackout.
Music.

LOUNGE BAR

MONAGH *on stage, at mike, glamorous.*

MONAGH   *(sings)* Though I can't explain
All the anger and the pain
Still I think you will agree with me
What's going on's insane
Houses open to the rain
Only misery and hate remain
But I for one, you and me for two,
Need to move on to something new . . .

During this, lights also come up on:

STREET

MARTYN *and* ROY *stand by a wall, with suitcases, confronting the* MAN *and* WOMAN *as a military police patrol.*

MAN   Hands on the wall. Feet apart.

They lean face-forward against the wall, as ordered. While the MAN *frisks them, the* WOMAN *searches their cases.*

Meanwhile the song continues.

MONAGH   *(singing)* All the world agrees
There's a cure for our disease

Just by helping one another
To get off our hands and knees

You know love can be the answer
You know love can show the way
Once we get ourselves together
There can be a brand new day

I for one, baby you and me for two,
Need to move, need to move to something new,
And I for one hope that you for one
Will travel that way too
'Cos I for one, baby you and me for two . . .

By now, the lights have faded out on the street search.
During the ensuing bridge, ROY *and* MARTYN *are seen*
entering the lounge bar and sitting down at a table.
The GIRL, *as a waitress, serves them drinks.*

. . . How we long to travel home
But home is something deep inside
We've lost our way
Home is just a place where we can hide away

I for one, baby you and me for two
Need to move, need to move to something new
So I for one hope that you for one
Will travel that way too
Yes, I for one, baby you and me for two,
I for one, baby you and me for two,
I for one, baby you and me for two,
And I for one hope that you for one
Will travel that way too.

MONAGH *bows and exits,* MARTYN *and* ROY *applauding.*

The MAN *enters, as a comedian, and takes the mike.*
He is dressed in scuba goggles and baggy shorts.
Round his waist is a gunbelt, with an old revolver in a
holster, and bottles of Guinness stuck in loops all the
way round.

MAN   Monagh Lisa, ladies and gents, Miss Monagh Lisa, a
       lovely lady from the black North, with a great future

ahead of her and a great behind as well, good evening! *(Fixes on* MARTYN *and* ROY*)*. Hey lads, tell us this, tell us the truth now—speaking as outsiders, what do you think of the human race? Eh? Did you ever consider surgery? You know, I met a fellow like you the other day, a Belfast lad. And he tells me he threw a grenade at an English soldier. My God, says I—what happened? Well, says your man—he just pulled out the pin from it and threw it straight back again. I'm a navy man myself, of course. You may laugh—it's been known to happen— but what you see standing here before you is the Irish Naval Services Anti-Submarine Patrol. That's me. Hang on, there's a message coming through from the interior. *(He flips the cap off a Guinness bottle and removes it from his belt)*. I don't have to do this, you know, I could work for a living. *(He takes a swig)*. You should try this under- water, lads, a different story altogether. Terrible trouble keeping your weapon dry, you'd know all about that of course. Anyway. The backroom boys came up with a great solution, look at this. *(He pulls out the revolver and squirts water at them)*. Isn't it rich? Isn't it good? Youse can sleep safe in your beds from now on, the two of youse. Snuggled up together. I'm away back to the frigate. I said frigate. Listen, I know there's somebody out there, I can hear breathing. Tomorrow you can hear me singing that evergreen favourite, 'I'll Be Seizing You In All The Old Familiar Places'—till then good night and good luck.

The band plays him off. The fluorescent pub lighting comes on, the band exits, chatting.

MARTYN *(looking around)* They're not doing very good business.
ROY You can see why.
MARTYN Monagh wasn't bad, though.
ROY She was singing our song.
  (Short pause)
MARTYN She mightn't have seen us.
ROY Couldn't have missed us.
MARTYN Maybe we should ask . . .
ROY Relax. She'll be changing.
MARTYN *(sings)* There's been a change in the weather and a change in me . . . *(Speaks)* How's the money?
ROY About thirty quid left.

MARTYN	We'll have to go home, Roy.
ROY	How can we go home? You want to get shot?
MARTYN	We can't sign on the dole down here, we're not citizens.
ROY	We're going to sell songs. We're going to write hits.
MARTYN	How long will thirty quid keep us alive?
ROY	Isn't there a month's rent paid on the bedsitter? *(Slight pause)*. You always have qualms. Could we just—once —enter into something—qualmlessly?
MARTYN	You're the one with the ulcer.
ROY	You're the one ordered the drinks.
MARTYN	You're the one with the cousin in the Protestant gestapo.
ROY	Give it a rest, will you? He plays the drums, that's all.
MARTYN	Just to keep in practice.
	(Pause)
	We must have been mental to write that stuff for him.
ROY	Will you quit grumping? It was a couple of parodies, a corny cabaret act they take round the drinking clubs. Nobody cares who writes the numbers so long as they go over well.
MARTYN	By God, that stuff should have gone over well. It curdled the ink in my ball-point.

MONAGH *rushes on in jeans and sweater.*

MONAGH	My public!
MARTYN	The star herself.
MONAGH	*(as she hugs them)* God, this is marvellous. You both look great.
MARTYN	We've been slimming.
ROY	You look pretty picturesque yourself.
MONAGH	Sure—with a name like Monagh Lisa.
MARTYN	Whose idea was that?
MONAGH	You'll meet her. Did you like the act?
MARTYN	It's a killer.
MONAGH	It's killing me, anyway.
ROY	So you want to go back to conducting the school choir?
MONAGH	Sure—in a coffin.
MARTYN	How did you get the job?
MONAGH	Blackmail. Prostitution. Murder. It was easy. How long are you down in Dublin for?
ROY	The duration.
MARTYN	We had to leave Belfast in a hurry. For a reason.
MONAGH	What was it?
ROY	Fear.

24

MARTYN	Somebody sent us these. *(He shows the two bullets)*.
MONAGH	Jesus Murphy. What have you been up to?
ROY	Nothing.
MARTYN	We wrote some material . . .
ROY	I'll tell you about it later!
MONAGH	Maybe it was Cochrane. Maybe it was Kyle.
ROY	No, we know it wasn't Marie.
MARTYN	British Army Intelligence. That's my theory.
ROY	Gunk.

The WOMAN *sweeps by as Mrs. Barker: tinted glasses. Cigarette. Glass of gin. An air of slightly slatternly superiority. Horsey baritone voice.*

WOMAN	I've told you before about fraternising, dear.
MONAGH	These are friends of mine from Belfast, Mrs. Barker . . . *(She makes a face at her departing back)*. We'll get a bus to my place. It's a rathole, but it's warm.
MARTYN	I think the rats have deserted ours.
WOMAN	*(re-appearing)* You'd swear I was running a charity. *(Sitting down, she drains her glass and holds it up to* MONAGH*)*. Tell Eamon to fill that for me, dear. You can bring something for your little friends, if you like.
MONAGH	Roy Fletcher. Martyn Semple. Mrs. Barker. *(They nod to each other)*. The usual?
ROY	Large.
MONAGH	Of course. *(She goes off)*
WOMAN	From the North, are you? Bloody silly place to live.
MARTYN	We've just moved, actually.
WOMAN	Good for you. How did you like my cabaret?
MARTYN	Very entertaining.
WOMAN	I could draw a bigger crowd with ballad sessions, but I can't stand that droning slush they all sing.
MARTYN	I know what you mean.
WOMAN	Of course the acts I'm forced to use are practically un-employable, but they do for the yokels here to gawp at. I suppose that's a Presbyterian name?
ROY	Pardon?
WOMAN	Ronald Fletcher, wasn't it?
MARTYN	Roy.
WOMAN	I'll tell you what I wish for you lot up North. I wish you'd get on with the bloody killing. Speed it up, hurry it along. Finish each other off, we'll be glad to see the

end of you, Protestants and Catholics both, you'll be doing the world a service.

MONAGH *re-appears with a tray containing the drinks.*

MONAGH Mrs. Barker has considerable experience in horse trials.

WOMAN She's such a pert little thing, I don't know why she's never managed to get herself a man.

MONAGH I didn't like to mention it before but I'm a female impersonator and this is my wife and mother-in-law *(she downs her drink).*

WOMAN I've told her often she'd have a much better chance as a comedienne. At least she's got a natural ability for that.

MONAGH She's never done flattering me.

WOMAN No point in pretending, dear. You're over the hill to start up as a pop singer. It might be different if you had, outstanding talent. But you don't even have decent tits, do you?

MONAGH Your own could do with a bit of re-pointing.

WOMAN Mine are no longer necessary, dear.

MONAGH Her husband was in the property market, you see—she inherited the Irish Stock Exchange.

WOMAN I suppose you two belong to Paisley's crew.

MARTYN We're not involved . . .

ROY I'm Protestant. He's Catholic. Satisfied?

WOMAN It's nothing to me, dear, the British are welcome to the whole crowd of you. I just hope they never try and fob you on to us.

MONAGH We wouldn't touch your kind with a green, white and orange barge-pole, dear.

MARTYN Monagh . . .

WOMAN You've crippled our tourism, you've blemished the name of Ireland throughout the world, and you're not even a part of it.
(Pause)

MONAGH What do you mean by that?

WOMAN I'm only stating facts, dear.

MONAGH I'm more Irish than you are, you overbearing old windbag!

ROY Cool down.

MONAGH She's not telling me I'm not Irish!

ROY What does it matter, who cares?

WOMAN You can label yourself with any name you like, dear, I'm talking about real life.

26

MONAGH	If you'd had a no-warning bomb in your fiberglass grotto here, you'd know all about real life, and hell slap it into you.
WOMAN	Don't be tiresome.
MARTYN	Easy on.
MONAGH	What does she know about it? What does she know about us? She's got no allegiance to anything except her cruddy cheque-book. *(To* WOMAN*)* You want to know why they're down here?
ROY	Let's go.
MONAGH	They got live bullets through the post! How'd you like that with your cornflakes?
MARTYN	Come on, Monagh, we're going home.
WOMAN	You're one of life's born losers, dear, and there's nothing more I can do for you.
MONAGH	You can stuff it up your horse-box for a start!
ROY	Out.

He manhandles her off. We hear her shouting: 'Piss off, I'm sick of this, sick of it, the old bitch' . . . etc.

MARTYN	Don't mind her, Mrs. Barker, she's overwrought.
WOMAN	She ought to know better than to take on a tough old boot like me.
MARTYN	First thing tomorrow morning, she'll be on the phone to apologise.
WOMAN	Tell her not to bother, dear. I'd already decided to drop her. Quite apart from her singing talent, she's a bloody awful entertainer. She won't stoop to sell herself. And you have to, dear. It's a whore's game at one remove.

She goes. Blackout.

MONAGH'S FLAT

In the darkness a television flickers on soundlessly, its back towards the audience. In the eerie fuzz of its light, MONAGH *is revealed on the sofa in front of it, watching.* ROY *enters with drinks. He gives her one, and leans on the back of the sofa, sipping.*

MONAGH	We should have waited for Martyn.

ROY	He'll soft-soap your woman, he's good at that.
MONAGH	I'm just sorry it had to happen five minutes after you arrived.
ROY	You can't afford to fall out with these people.
MONAGH	That's her way of getting rid of everybody—needling them till they blow their tops.
ROY	It was a nice little gig to have.
MONAGH	God! The back of my neck to my kidneys is just one long throb.

ROY *puts down his drink and begins massaging her neck and shoulders.*

Aah . . . sublime.

She closes her eyes and he continues for a moment in silence, watching the television.

ROY	What *is* this?
MONAGH	Some documentary about the troubles.
ROY	They never give it a rest, do they? *(He watches, still massaging).* That's near Cecilia Street, I went to school there.
MONAGH	Not much of it left now.
ROY	Look—that was that bar off York Street.
MONAGH	That's the Dublin Road.
ROY	Is it?
MONAGH	Oh God knows, I've lost track. When will it ever end?
ROY	You don't have to watch it.
MONAGH	It won't just go away if you switch it off, you know.
ROY	It'll not be stopped by wallowing in it either. *(He stops massaging).* How's that?
MONAGH	You haven't lost the touch.
ROY	It's grown more sensitive over the years.
MONAGH	With practice, no doubt.

He moves round the sofa to her side.

ROY	It's a gift of nature. *(He makes to kiss her).*
MONAGH	Hold on, Roy, this wasn't included in my five-year plan.
ROY	Come on, Monagh . . . *(he reaches for her).*
MONAGH	Sit down. *(She pushes him on to the sofa).* It isn't real, what's happening to us, I can't keep track. We'd all been drifting along teaching for seven years. The next

	thing you know, Kyle's running around with bombs, you and Martyn are a pair of hunted balladmongers, and I'm getting the bums' rush from a lounge bar.
ROY	Listen, sprite. Something fell into place tonight.
MONAGH	You haven't called me 'sprite' for five years.
ROY	Listen to me. You were good tonight. Real charisma.
MONAGH	You're fantasising, Roy.
ROY	It took me completely unawares. You knocked me out.
MONAGH	Are you trying to talk your way into bed?
ROY	Not unless that's the price of admission.
MONAGH	There are five thousand singers better than me in this town alone, and that's not counting the ones over sixteen.
ROY	Look, will you forget this neurosis about age, the youth cult's a thing of the past. There's a huge maturity market now.
MONAGH	Sounds like the fatstock sales. Where do you get these phrases from?
ROY	All I'm trying to suggest is—why don't the three of us work as a team? We can develop a whole strategy together, a concept. An image.
MONAGH	You mean, like you write the songs and I sing them?
ROY	We co-ordinate everything—writing, singing, clothes, records, marketing, promotion. We aim the whole thing towards television. That's where we ultimately score.
MONAGH	Gee, kids—let's just do the show ourselves!
ROY	Monagh Enterprises.
MONAGH	Right here in this battered old country.
ROY	What do you say?
MONAGH	I was going to play a game with myself for five years. Sing around the clubs and hotels. Live a bit wild. Get out of the old necropolis. *(She gestures towards the television)*. Take a vacation from real life. You can't, of course. That was my five-year plan.
ROY	Scrap it, sprite. We're going for the Great Leap Forward. *(He kisses her on the lips, then on the ear, then the shoulder. Meanwhile, her attention is caught by the television programme again)*.
MONAGH	Bloody English politicians . . .
ROY	Ah, hell's teeth!
MONAGH	Look at them, they're always so sanctimonious. They get on like a crowd of doctors. It never seems to sink in that they're part of the disease.
ROY	Could this maybe wait, do you think?

MONAGH	They treat us like some remote tribe of savages.
ROY	They're not far wrong.
MONAGH	So that's your considered opinion of your fellow-citizens?
ROY	It's got nothing to do with me, all that gunk there.
MONAGH	Apart from earning yourself a bullet in the mail.
ROY	Ah, come off it.
MONAGH	Who sent them, Roy?
ROY	Search me—some clown probably got the address wrong.

They get engrossed in the television programme again.

MONAGH	What's that?
ROY	M.I. Carbine.
MONAGH	You'd think it was a form of sport they were dealing with. There's an Armalite rifle.

They're watching footage of a gun battle. MONAGH *winches and looks away.*

	How does little Marie Kyle live with all that? She's in the thick of it. I can barely watch it on television. She was always such a mouse. I was supposed to be the hard-bitten woman of the world.
ROY	She was born with blinkers on, same as the rest of them.
MONAGH	All except Roy Fletcher, mighty man of steel.
ROY	Knock it off.
MONAGH	You really hate your country, don't you?
ROY	I can think of better places to be born.
MONAGH	Too late now, sprite, you're stuck with it, and you better start facing up to the fact. *(Pause)*. Are you staying the night?
ROY	I want to.
MONAGH	Just don't kid yourself we're a winning concept.
ROY	It's the old firm. In earnest this time. I still love you, Monagh.
MONAGH	Excuse me for calling in question one or two of your terms, Mr. Fletcher. 'Still' for example. And 'you'. And particularly 'love'. And of course 'I'.
ROY	Just give me a chance.
MONAGH	Certainly. Let's twist again like we did last summer. *(Pause)*
ROY	I suppose this is one of Playfair's programmes.
MONAGH	Why so?

ROY You seemed in quite a hurry to switch it on.

MONAGH We can dispense with that sort of crack for a start. We're in the maturity market now, right? That's where we all make our own breakfast and find our own way home. Okay?
(Pause)
You really liked the act?

ROY I thought you were sensational.

She kisses him. He reaches for her.

MONAGH Wait.

She switches the television off. Blackout.

A recording of Monagh singing 'I for One' fades in towards the end of the song. Then a disc jockey voice is heard saying: 'A first record there from a lady by the name of Monagh, with a number called "I For One" which I for one rather fancy myself, here's hoping you for one like it too for one. The time coming up to nine forty, the weather cold and cloudy, but stay tuned for more of the best in music . . .' *The song is faded up again as it comes to an end.*

AGENT'S OFFICE

Lights up on the MAN, *as a booking agent, sitting at a desk.* MONAGH *standing on the other side of it.*

MAN Monagh, my sweet, look at you, you're a walking talking daydream. Come here and make an old man happy. *(He kisses her cheek).* My God, you're a public incitement to divorce.

MONAGH Did you ever just try saying hello, Cyril?

MAN No oul' lip now, I've got two bookings for you, and I expect you to show grateful, sit down there and look demure.

MONAGH Is it television?

MAN A television spot for new talent plus a live variety spot and it adds up to good money. How's the two boyos?

MONAGH Eager to please, Cyril. Tell me about the television.

31

MAN	They're hard-working lads and they're sound and you know what—they should be trying their stuff in the Song Festivals. You tell them from me—Song Festivals.
MONAGH	They've entered a number in the National Contest for Eurovision.
MAN	Certainly Eurovision, but there's plenty of smaller fry besides. There's Castlebar in this country, there's loads of them on the continent, Majorca, Knokke-la-Zoute, Monte Carlo, you tell them from me, there's money in it.
MONAGH	What's the live gig, Cyril?
MAN	Now it sounds not—very—exciting, but it's a first-class bill of professional artistes and, believe me, very well respected as a booking in the business. It's a Christmas Night concert in the Women's Prison.
MONAGH	Good God. How did this come about? I suppose you've a lot of business colleagues in there?
MAN	Any more of this cheek and I'll give the booking to my sword-swallowing act.
MONAGH	I'm not ungrateful. I'm just wondering what they do to you if they don't like your performance.
MAN	Sure it's full of those Republican girls from Belfast—they'll be delighted with you and your act.
MONAGH	Captivated, in fact.
MAN	My God, what a wit.
MONAGH	So what about the *good* news, the television?
MAN	From what I've been told, it's a showcase series for new performers, professional, all professional—and you're on the first one. Can those fellows of yours come up with the right sort of song, do you think?
MONAGH	I'll make damn sure they do.

Blackout.

ROY AND MARTYN'S FLAT

Light up on ROY *sitting at an old upright piano, improvising moodily.*

ROY   What have you got?

Light up on MARTYN *downstage in a rocking chair, smoking a pipe, leafing through a big notebook.*

MARTYN	Not a lot. Fallen Arches. A song for broken-hearted chiropodists.
ROY	Where did that thing come from?
MARTYN	I bought it this morning.
ROY	You don't smoke.
MARTYN	I thought I'd give it a try.
ROY	It looks ridiculous.
	(He plays some gloomy chords and runs)
MARTYN	I've been toying with the theme of a secret agent. Espionage.
ROY	You've got spies on the brain.
MARTYN	My lover . . . works undercover, kind of thing.
ROY	Sounds obscene.
MARTYN	He dresses to kill, gives me my fill. That sort of idea. His shoes are made from an alligator. He shoots first and asks questions later.
ROY	We're not writing for Bessie Smith.
MARTYN	True. *(He doodles)*. Nobody's likely to track us down here. I can't even remember the address myself half the time. *(He doodles more)*. I mean, who would send a death threat on account of a few ballads?
ROY	Will you quit talking about it?
MARTYN	Secret society. Swear an oath that you'll be true. Learn the password—I love you.
ROY	The demo tape came back again, incidentally.
MARTYN	Thanks but no thanks?
ROY	They're interested—songs show promise—not quite out of the ordinary enough—try them again—they remain ours etc.
MARTYN	What about trying London?
ROY	No, that tape's had its chance. We're just not in focus yet. We need stuff that's ballady and romantic—plus a dash of drama.
MARTYN	Secret heart.
ROY	She's good at drama, she thrives on it.
MARTYN	Secret sorrow . . . secret joy . . . secret love . . . that's been done.
ROY	Keep going.
	(He doodles on the piano)
MARTYN	My heart has its orders . . . from up above . . . a top-secret mission . . . to win your love . . . no, to capture your love . . . de-dah-dah-dum . . . something our engagement . . . then I found out . . . you're a double agent!

ROY	You keep coming out with these duff gag lines.
MARTYN	That's not a gag. It's wit.
ROY	We don't need wit. We're creating a product for a nation of half-wits.
MARTYN	How *is* Monagh, anyway?
ROY	She was late for the gig again last night.
MARTYN	Have you been tiring her out?
ROY	Fat chance. She treats me like a brand of convenience food. Just pop it in the oven for fifteen minutes, when you're feeling peckish, ladies.
MARTYN	Sounds ideal.
ROY	Well, that's not how it feels. She's cold-bloodedly destroying me, if you want to know. You and her both seem to think that I'm some kind of a mechanical robot.
MARTYN	Small wonder, the way you get on.

ROY *looks over his shoulder at* MARTYN. *They stare at one another for a moment.*

ROY	Say that again.
MARTYN	Small wonder . . . it's tearing me asunder.
ROY	Right. We're in business.

The lights stay on them as they work quietly away at the idea.

TELEVISION STUDIO

Lights up on MONAGH, *facing a television camera; the* MAN *is the cameraman. The* GIRL, *as a floor manager, enters wearing a headset and carrying a clipboard.*

GIRL	We're ready to go now, love. Just do it bit by bit the way I said, while he lines up his shots. I'll give you a hand cue to start and stop. Okay?

MONAGH *nods. The* GIRL *cues her to start. Music.*

MONAGH	*(sings)* I have seen the cover
	That you've been living under
	To leave your former lovers high and dry . . .
GIRL	*(signalling)* Fine, love. Keep your position.

34

They wait.

FLAT

MARTYN   *(looking up in the air)* Small wonder . . . what does it apply to? My Small Wonder. A song for midgets.

ROY   This could be the one to break her, you know. I've a feeling it might.

MARTYN   Oh small wonder, you and I . . .

ROY   You need a romantic ballad to break nearly any female act.

MARTYN   . . . *No* small wonder, you and I.

ROY   It just needs some sort of twist, to make it really commercial.

MARTYN   Play me what you've got.

ROY   *(playing and singing)* Oh, small wonder . . . *(Speaks)* That's all.

MARTYN   That's the hook.

They go back to work.

TELEVISION STUDIO

GIRL   Ready.

She cues music and MONAGH.

MONAGH   *(sings)* In disguise, small wonder,
For each time we're together
Every girl around
Gives you the eye . . .

GIRL   *(signalling)* Hold.

They wait.

FLAT

MARTYN   Wonder. Wonder. The seven wonders of the world. There must be something there. The eighth wonder.

35

Oh, small wonder, the eighth one . . . no, *call our wonder*
the eighth one of the world . . . We can . . . do what?
We can fly . . . no, we can reach so high. Higher . . .
than the sky. No small wonder you and I! Genius!

TELEVISION STUDIO

The GIRL *cues* MONAGH *and the music.*

MONAGH   *(sings)* You've given yourself away
                    You've said too much that I
                    Can read between the lines
                    Your face and hands complete the picture —

                    Oh, small wonder,
                    You and I,
                    Meeting in the park, touching in the dark —

                    Call our wonder
                    The eighth one of the world
                    We can reach so high
                    Higher than the sky
                    No small wonder, you and I . . .
GIRL   *(signalling)* Is there much more of it, love?
MONAGH   Fifty whole percent.
GIRL   Well, catch your breath for a couple of minutes.

FLAT

ROY   *(still at the piano)* I know what Monagh's problem is
       now. She can't cope with being a free agent. She can't
       handle it. That's why she does all these lame things. So
       as somebody'll rush up and give her a hand. She acts
       the self-reliant woman but she's crying inside for some-
       body to run her life for her. Trouble is, it's not me. It's
       that television jock, Playfair. She's still hooked on that
       creep. She's just using me as a home help.
MARTYN   Okay, I've got a lead on the verse.
ROY   What about the chorus?
MARTYN   It's finished.

36

ROY   It's only started.

MARTYN   You never listen!

ROY   All I hear is you sitting there mumbling to yourself.

MARTYN   I'm only after going through the whole thing.

ROY   Where is it?

     MARTYN *tears a page from his notebook, plants it down on the piano and returns to his seat.*

MARTYN   It'll sweep the country, this. From the jukebox in every sleazy waterfront drive . . . to the ballroom in every Fifth Avenue hotel. *(Pause)* Will Monagh like it, do you think?

ROY   She doesn't like anything much. Except that turd Playfair. He can do no wrong.

MARTYN   I thought it was over years ago.

ROY   She says he wanted a divorce. But the wife wouldn't play along. And so on and so forth. You wouldn't think a woman of her intelligence would fall for that. But she wants to badly enough. So she does. Bitch. *(He fights his distress)*. What about the verse?

MARTYN   Shaping up. Spies may be all round us, jealously may hound us.

ROY   You and your bloody spies!

MARTYN   Watching for the signs that say we're through. Some day they may discover . . . love has got our number . . . and even something something can come true . . . miracles! And even miracles are sometimes true. Bullseye!

ROY   Bullshit.

TELEVISION STUDIO

GIRL   *(cueing)* Go.

     Music

MONAGH   *(sings)* Spies may be all round us
          Jealousy may hound us
          Watching for the signs that say we're through
          One day they may discover
          Love has got our number
          And even miracles are sometimes true . . .

37

The GIRL *signals to stop. They wait.*

FLAT

> ROY, *with tears on his cheeks, gets up suddenly and heads for the door.*

MARTYN   Where're you going?
ROY   I'm going for a walk.
MARTYN   That's only the half of it.

> ROY *leaves,* MARTYN *sighs, and grimaces with exasperation. Then gets engrossed again.*

Making me your bride. Nothing left to hide. Live life side by side. *(Pause).* Assuming you prefer your onions fried.

> *Blackout on flat.*

TELEVISION STUDIO

GIRL   Straight through to the end now.

> *She cues* MONAGH

MONAGH   *(sings)*   You've given yourself away
You've said too much that I
Can read between the lines
Your face and hands complete the picture —

Oh, small wonder,
You and I,
Meeting in the park, touching in the dark,
Call our wonder
The eighth one of the world
We can reach so high
Higher than the sky
No small wonder, you and I.

GIRL   Okay. Lunch!

> *Blackout on television studio.*

38

> MARTYN *is looking through some poetry collections.*
> MARIE *enters.*

MARIE Surprise.

MARTYN Marie!

MARIE So this is where you've run to?

MARTYN What are you doing here?

MARIE Visiting friends. Selling books. What about you? Here. *(She gives him a Sinn Fein pamphlet from her satchel).* Thirty pence, please.

MARTYN Roy and me are getting established, with the songs. We've got a couple of records out, with Monagh. We're doing an entry for Eurovision at the minute. Listen, I'm sorry about the ballad. We had to leave Belfast in a bit of a rush.

MARIE Very wise. I'm surprised at what's become of you, Semple.

MARTYN Me?

MARIE Fletcher always was a wee Orange pimp, under the skin.

MARTYN Easy on, Marie.

MARIE You're in his pocket, that's the thing. I thought you told me your grandfather carried a gun in the twenties.

MARTYN The past is over and done with, Marie. We're in the Common Market now.

MARIE You amuse me.

MARTYN Men have been on the moon. It's a small world.

MARIE Don't delude yourself, you can't just turn your back on generations of the dead. Don't imagine you'll get away with it that easy.

MARTYN I'm in favour of a united Ireland as much as the next man.

MARIE What are you doing reproducing this pseudo-American slop, then?

MARTYN What? What has that got to do with it?

MARIE Everything, that's all. The whole state apparatus of this country, North and South, is designed for one function— sell-out. Selling out the resources, the heritage, the culture, the very soil itself to foreign speculators.

MARTYN Come off it.

MARIE You're a cog in that machine, you and your Common Market and your Eurovision Song Contest.

MARTYN For God's sake, Marie, that's completely wired up.

39

	I mean, people enjoying songs, a harmless entertainment . . .
MARIE	Nothing that mediocre is ever harmless.
MARTYN	You've lost touch with real life.
MARIE	You've lost touch with who and what and where you are. Don't think you can escape for ever into mass-produced catchpenny idiocies.
MARTYN	Pop songs are like the folk music of our generation. There's nothing political about it.
MARIE	That's really rich, coming from you, in your position.
MARTYN	What are you talking about?
MARIE	I'm talking about why you did a flit.
MARTYN	Somebody posted bullets to us.
MARIE	You're damn lucky they didn't arrive at a higher velocity.
MARTYN	Why do you say that?
MARIE	Considering what you were mixed up in.
MARTYN	Us? We'd no involvement in politics whatsoever as you know.
MARIE	Don't act all innocent. You took to the wing the minute it appeared in print.
MARTYN	Whatever you're on about, Marie . . . I think maybe I'd rather not know.
MARIE	You're not bluffing, are you—you really don't know what you've got yourself into. There was an article in a Protestant paper. Naming you two. It said you'd both been supplying entertainment to their drinking clubs. As a means of gaining information about them. On behalf of the British Army. The proof was that you were also doing work for the I.R.A. You're in dead trouble, Martyn.
MARTYN	But none of it's true!
MARIE	Oh? You did no work for the Protestants, then?
MARTYN	We wrote a few comedy numbers for a cousin of Roy's, that's all.
MARIE	You're the original babes in the wood, aren't you?
MARTYN	What'll happen? What should we do?
MARIE	These things aren't forgotten.
MARTYN	We literally didn't know. I suppose there's no point in even trying to refute it now.
MARIE	Not much.
MARTYN	Good God, Marie, surely *you* never believed it?
MARIE	I wouldn't put anything past Fletcher, but I was sceptical all the same. Even the Brits have more gumption than

	to employ the likes of you.
MARTYN	I can't get over it.
MARIE	Well, the best of British luck, as they say. I hope it's got more to offer than British justice.

MARTYN	I can't get over it.
MARIE	Well, the best of British luck, as they say. I hope it's got more to offer than British justice.

MARTYN   I can't get over it.

MARIE   Well, the best of British luck, as they say. I hope it's got more to offer than British justice.

(She makes to leave).

MARTYN   Don't run off—what about a drink?

MARIE   Sorry—I've another three shops to go round.

MARTYN   See that girl over there?

MARIE   What about her?

MARTYN   Just before you came in, she shouts up to the woman at the cash register—Audrey . . . where the hell's the Savage Mind? I thought it would make a beautiful skit. Two assistants shouting across the heads of the customers—Where's the Female Eunuch? I don't know, but there's a couple of Trollopes under the counter . . . *(She smiles).* You remember the old college revues?

MARIE   Of course I do, why wouldn't I?

MARTYN   You were some stage manager.

MARIE   You were some comedian.

MARTYN   We put in a lot of happy days and nights together, Marie.

MARIE   It was half a lifetime ago.

MARTYN   Seven years, that's all.

MARIE   Some seven years.

MARTYN   It's tragic to let it just completely vanish, all the same.

MARIE   You have to grow up sometime, Martyn.

MARTYN   You've time for a quick jar, come on.

MARIE   No. I'm away. Incidentally, the Irish History section's over there.

She leaves. MARTYN, *left alone, tears the pamphlet in half. Blackout.*

PRISON HALL

The band plays the introduction to 'Somebody Out There'. Light up on the WOMAN, *as a prison governess.*

WOMAN   Since the proceedings are now drawing to a close, I think the time has come for me to express the appreciation of all inmates and staff to our show-business guests for coming here tonight. You've given most generously of your time and talents to bring the pleasure of good enter-

41

tainment into our lives, and I can assure you on behalf of all the inmates most especially of how much this kind of thing means to them. But I think you'll find them ready to express their gratitude for themselves in the customary manner, in just a moment. We all hope to see you back with us again soon—in your professional capacities, of course. And now for the last item on the agenda *(she consults a piece of paper)* a song by Monagh, her latest one, which I'm sure we all hope will do very well.

Music. Follow spot on MONAGH *entering.*

MONAGH *(sings)* Somebody out there loves you, sugar,
Somebody out there wants to know you
Give them your smile, give them the eye,
They'll run a mile to be your girl or guy
Somebody in here needs some friendship
Somebody in here wants to love you
Don't be afraid of it
You can make the grade of it
Someone in there can surely see
That the somebody out here is me!

Lights come up on ROY *and* MARTYN *in their flat, singing the song at the piano.*

Life can be hard
Times can be lean
Life can get lonely too
But don't give up
Don't get mad
Don't be had
Because there's somebody out there
Yes, there's somebody out there
Yes, there's somebody out there
Somebody out there . . .

The lights have narrowed down to two small pools, one on Monagh's face, the other on Roy and Martyn's faces. They all three stare fearfully out into the surrounding darkness, as they sing the final repeated line.

Blackout. END OF ACT ONE

ACT TWO

ROY AND MARTYN'S FLAT

> ROY *sitting in an armchair leafing through a contract.*
> MARTYN *preparing to photograph him. Table set for
> dinner.*

ROY   We're on our way, Sempo. No question about it.

MARTYN   Hold it.

> *He takes the photograph.* MONAGH *enters with a soup
> tureen.*

ROY   Fletcher and Semple. Hereinafter referred to as the composer/author of the one part.

MONAGH   Soup. *(She's ladling it out).*

MARTYN   Nifty machine, isn't it? *(The camera).*

ROY   Look at that beautiful document.

MARTYN   The Rolls Royce of cameras, these are.

MONAGH   Soup!

ROY   Oh, right. *(He goes to the table).*

MARTYN   The man in the shop was telling me.

ROY   Sit down.

> MARTYN *sits. They all three eat their soup.*

MARTYN   What time tomorrow?

ROY   Ten a.m. sharp in his office. Hereinafter referred to as the publisher of the other part.

MARTYN   They wouldn't just sit on the songs?

ROY   They'll be sending the demos all over. I'm telling you. From now on we're a brand name, in with the big ones.

MONAGH   Oh, for the love of God!

ROY   What's up?

MONAGH   Will you please talk about something other than cursed songs! Just for once! There's a whole world to choose from.
(Strained pause while they eat their soup).

ROY   Any news from home?

MARTYN   Home?

ROY   How's your mother?

MARTYN   My mother?

ROY   Is she keeping well?

MARTYN	I dunno.
	(Pause)
ROY	That was a nasty business over the weekend.
MARTYN	What was?
ROY	The bombing.
MARTYN	Which one?
ROY	You watched it with me on T.V.
MARTYN	The big fire?
ROY	The bombing!
MONAGH	*(getting up, clearing soup bowls)* I can hardly bear to tear myself away from this.

She goes off.

ROY	Bitch.
MARTYN	I think she feels left out.
ROY	She won't even let up for a celebration.
MARTYN	Did I show you the book of desert photographs I bought?
ROY	Yeah, you did. *(He starts browsing through the contract again)*.
MARTYN	Stunning lunar effects.
ROY	Sure. The language here's really historical. Look at this. *(He reads)*. '. . . in respect of gramophone records, piano rolls and all other devices for audibly reproducing the said work for sale or hire in the United Kingdom of Great Britain and Northern Ireland, and the Republic of Ireland . . .'.

MONAGH has re-appeared with a steaming chicken which she dumps on the table.

MONAGH	How about carving the said chicken.

She goes off again. ROY *puts the contract in his pocket, gets up, and starts to cut into the thigh of the chicken.*

MARTYN	I think you'll like the wine I've chosen.
ROY	This is tough.
MARTYN	It's young but it's got quite a lot of body. *(He goes off to get it)*.
ROY	Yeccch . . .

MONAGH re-appears with plates.

MONAGH	What's wrong?
ROY	It's all bloody inside.
MONAGH	What do you mean?
ROY	It's all red.
MONAGH	It's been roasting for hours.
ROY	We can't eat that. Was it frozen?
MONAGH	*(sings)* Don't get the bird—Get Brady's!

Pop! As MARTYN, *re-entering, draws the cork from the wine.*

ROY	You mustn't have thawed it out fully.
MONAGH	You're the expert, of course. You wrote the jingle for the commercial, you would know all about it.
ROY	I'm only pointing out the obvious.
MONAGH	You've a genuine talent for that.
ROY	We'd better put it back in the oven.
MONAGH	Carve it up. We're eating it.
ROY	It's raw inside.
MONAGH	It's medium rare.
ROY	It's still bleeding!
MONAGH	Give me.

She grabs the carving knife and fork from him and begins hacking at the chicken.

ROY	You can get food poisoning that way, you know. It's stupid. You needn't carve any for me, I'm not eating that.
MONAGH	Shut your hole!

She grabs the chicken and flings it at him. It hits him in the chest, but he catches it and juggles it from hand to hand back on to the plate. Then he clamps his burnt hands to his sides under his armpits, and bends over in pain.

MONAGH	It's all yours! If you don't want to eat it you can always set it to music!

She storms out. MARTYN *holds up the wine bottle.*

MARTYN	Châteauneuf du Pape. Last year's.
ROY	I won't be able to play the piano.

MARTYN	Keep the air off them. Here, I've a couple of hankies. Give me.

ROY extends his right hand, keeping the left under his arm. MARTYN bandages the palm.

ROY	That's why she did it, she's trying to wreck my career.
MARTYN	Maybe we should have gone out for a meal after all.
ROY	What'll we do about Friday?
MARTYN	She'll have cooled off by then.
ROY	I'm talking about me!
MARTYN	Other hand please.

ROY extends his left hand and MARTYN bandages it.

ROY	How am I going to play?
MARTYN	Sure the keyboard tracks are already recorded.
ROY	So they are. So they are. Thank God. That's a piece of luck.
MARTYN	It's going to be an enormous number, wait till you see.

He finishes bandaging, and pours some wine.

ROY	I don't know what I'm supposed to do.
MARTYN	Have you ever thought of composing something personal? *(He hands ROY a wine glass).* Expressing the pain of your own feelings? In musical form?
ROY	I make no demands. Whatsoever. None.
MARTYN	Something like a rhapsody. Or a fantasia.
ROY	What do *you* think I should do?
MARTYN	I've been thinking about it for some time now, Roy. Why don't we write a concept album?
ROY	I'm not talking about bloody music, I'm talking about Monagh and me! *(He swills down the wine. Pause. MARTYN sips).*
MARTYN	Really quite fruity, yes?
ROY	I want help, I want advice, I want to hear what I'm supposed to do.
MARTYN	How do I know?
ROY	You're the one with the divorce. *(Pause)*
MARTYN	We made an agreement never to talk about that.
ROY	I don't recall signing that one.
MARTYN	There was an understanding.

ROY	Well, it's just been buggered. I'm a war victim, I'm in no mood to observe the niceties. You've been through all this, there must be something you've learnt.
MARTYN	If you wanted advice on passing exams, you wouldn't go to the village idiot, would you?
ROY	You've never bothered much with women since it, have you?
MARTYN	Abstinence makes the heart grow stronger.
ROY	You never even try to score.
MARTYN	At least I've still got skin on my hands.
ROY	What the hell did she do to you—bite it off?
MARTYN	She didn't seem to agree with me, and the subject's closed.
ROY	You must still get the itch, so what do you do about it?
MARTYN	Hold it under a cold tap.
ROY	I want to know.
MARTYN	What's the odds.
ROY	I want to know what you do about sex!
MARTYN	What do you think, I take care of it myself. *(Pause)*
ROY	Jerk off, you mean?
MARTYN	My hands and I are consenting adults. What passes between us in private is our own little affair.
ROY	Jerking off—that's repulsive.
MARTYN	Your whole sexual vocabulary's repulsive.
ROY	How can you do it? It's disgusting.
MARTYN	It's right up to date. Fast. Efficient. Hygienic. Available twenty-four hours a day. No fuss. No complications. Everybody does it.
ROY	I don't bloody do it.
MARTYN	You're a romantic idealist. The last one still alive.
ROY	I've got the same needs and appetites as any other normal healthy man . . .
MARTYN	And what a wonderful advertisement for them you make. Just at the moment. *(He indicates the chicken)*. A morsel of roast flesh?

ROY *grimaces.* MARTYN *takes a piece and eats it, sipping the wine.*

MARTYN	Love At First Smite. A song for masochists.

The introduction to the music of 'Aren't You the Lucky One' starts. The lights on ROY *and* MARTYN *fade out.*

> *The strip-lighting comes on.* MONAGH *is standing inside a recording booth, wearing headphones. Grouped around the microphone in a downstage corner is the vocal trio, who sing backing harmonies. Their voices are heard au naturel, but those of* MONAGH, MARTYN *and* ROY *are heard through the studio speakers. The music stops abruptly.*

ROY   *(off)* All right, are you all quite happy enough out there?

TRIO   Sure. Yes. Fine.

ROY   Monagh?

MONAGH   Never jollier.

ROY   Okay. Stand by. Here we go.

> *The music starts.*

MONAGH   *(sings)* He called on the phone,
He told me how everyone
Hoped I'd be there,
For I was so droll, the life and the soul
Of each social affair,
I dressed in my finery, played to the gallery,
A queen on her throne,
But then he smiled and went to the corner where
You sat alone
But
Oh my, I was the lucky one,
They all wanted to be by my side,
While you were left as the lonely one
In the shadows it's easy to hide
But nobody knows how I'm crying besides . . .
(speaks) Oh shit! I just can't sing this po-faced drivel!

> *The music stops.* MONAGH *bursts out of the booth.*

MONAGH   *(to the Vocal Trio)* I'm sorry, folks.

GIRL   Never fret, love.

MONAGH   I knew I'd bungle that shagging line. I could feel it coming.

WOMAN   It's a mouthful.

ROY, *hands still bandaged, enters from the cubicle followed by* MARTYN.

ROY   Now listen, everything's basically fine . . .
MONAGH *(still to the Trio)* That's good to hear, isn't it. And there was us thinking that maybe, after several hundred bungled takes, things were getting a teeny bit fraught.
ROY   We're nearly home.
MONAGH *(still to the Trio)* It's like chewing feathers, inside that booth.
ROY   It was going well. It just needs—livening up.
MONAGH *(to the* MAN*)* Do you like this number?
MAN   I can't remember.
MONAGH It gives me the runs.
ROY   *(to* MARTYN*)* You talk to her.
        (He goes)
MARTYN If you'll just do the last verse again, the engineer can drop you in for it.
MONAGH Thank God for that.
MARTYN Try singing it this time.
MONAGH Try lighting your fire with it next time.

She goes back into the booth. MARTYN *exits.*

ROY   *(off)* We'll play you into the last verse, then. Stand by.

The music comes up.

MONAGH *(singing deadpan)*
                You told me you envied me,
                Footloose and fancy-free,
                Loved and admired
                For you felt insecure, so shy and unsure of what
                Others desired,
                The party was breaking up,
                The morning was waking up,
                I still couldn't leave
                And then he came and whispered and led you a-
                Way by the sleeve
                But
                Oh my, I was the lucky one,
                They all wanted to be by my side
                While you were left as the lonely one
                In the shadows it's easy to hide,

But nobody knows how I'm crying inside
Because it was you that he chose for his bride—
You know it's funny but true—
Aren't you the lucky one too
Aren't you the lucky one too
Aren't you the lucky one too.

The lights have gradually reduced to a single one on
MONAGH *in the booth, which blacks out at the end of*
the song. Meanwhile, ROY *and* MARTYN, *with overcoats*
on, are seen entering a pub and sitting on stools.

PUB

MARTYN	Tragic.
ROY	It's all because of Playfair, he has her demented.
MARTYN	Time for reappraisals, Roy.
ROY	Don't fret, she'll grow out of it.
MARTYN	It's not just Monagh, it's the whole conundrum. We always seem to be on the run, I need to find some bearings.
ROY	Meaning what?
MARTYN	We're living here and now. Ireland in the seventies. I want to try and feel at home with that.
ROY	Once we've made it, you'll feel at home with the universe.
MARTYN	I'm talking about intangibles. Sensibility. Identity. Actually, I've been meaning to mention this to you for some time. I'm putting together a volume of verse for publication. *(Pause)*
ROY	You've never really stopped being an English teacher, have you?
MARTYN	Sneer. Go ahead. You're an inverted snob.
ROY	You should be devoting every working hour to songs, same as I do.
MARTYN	The songs have just become a job for me. Let's be honest, they're only ephemeral trivia. I want to write something important, something about real life.
ROY	We're not going progressive at this stage.
MARTYN	You know what we are? We're pushers. We're dealing in mild narcotics. *(With dramatic emphasis)*. We're the bland leading the bland.

50

ROY   What have you been reading?

MARTYN   There's more to life than that, Roy.

ROY   Listen, we're in business selling a legitimate product like any other law-abiding citizen. We're putting together decent commercial songs without any artsy-fartsy pretensions—and we're going to work at it till we get to the top.

MARIE KYLE *has entered with the* GIRL, *as a friend, in tow.*

MARTYN   Hello, Marie.

MARIE   You'd swear there was one of us following the other.

MARTYN   What brings you here?

MARIE   We've been doing a radio programme.

ROY   I thought your crowd was banned from the air.

MARIE   An Irish language programme. So far as I know we're still allowed to breathe the air.

ROY   It's a pity you don't extend that right to your victims.

MARTYN   *(hastily)* Monagh's just been recording one of our numbers for a radio show.

MARIE   Children's Hour, is it?

ROY   She's doing another prison concert next week, with a bit of luck you'll be able to attend it.

MARTYN   Listen. We used to be good chums. The four of us. The old college gang.

MARIE   Where have you been for the last seven years? The country's been at war, you know, a lot of chums are in prison. A lot of chums of mine have given their lives.

MARTYN   The thing of it is—Roy and I just aren't politically involved.

ROY   We don't swallow the sort of fanatical gunk that you use to justify murder.

MARIE   I know where I stand. On eight hundred years of history, eight hundred years of repression, exploitation and attempted genocide . . .

ROY   I live in the twentieth century, love.

MARIE   . . . this time we're going to put an end to that for all time. There's unfinished business in this country . . .

ROY   You know, the twentieth century—aeroplanes, spin dryers. Pinball machines.

MARIE   . . . and you're involved as much as any other Irishman which is right up over your ears whether you want to be or not.

ROY   You can keep your history. You belong in it. They should build museums for you instead of prisons. The

rest of us want shot of it.
(To MARTYN*)* Let's go.

He leaves.

MARTYN   I mean, we could still be friends, without having to
           agree about all this. We used to just discuss it over a
           beer.
MARIE   You're both like two spoiled brats! Irresponsible
           children!
MARTYN   *(going)* You've let yourself get bitter, Marie.

He leaves.

MARIE   *(shouting after them)* There's fifteen thousand British
           troops fighting an imperialist war on the soil of your
           own country! When are you going to wake up? What
           are you going to do about it?

She walks off with her friend. Blackout.

STREET

The GIRL, *as Playfair's wife, is standing smoking a
cigarette, waiting.* MONAGH *appears.*

GIRL   *(extending her hand)* I'm Sylvia Playfair, Miss Cahoon.
           Thank you for agreeing to meet me.
           (Pause)
MONAGH   I'd like to sit down somewhere.
GIRL   No, I'd sooner just say my piece and be off. *(Pause).* I
           want you to stop seeing my husband. He himself wishes
           to end the affair, but he can't bring himself to hurt your
           feelings. So the initiative has to come from you, I'm
           afraid.
           (Pause)
MONAGH   You're being frightfully British about this.
GIRL   I don't enjoy . . .
MONAGH   Did he send you here?
GIRL   The sole reason I'm here is that you're distracting him
           from his work. As you know, he's the only broadcaster
           in Belfast who's trusted by both sides. What you don't

52

know is that he's been acting as a go-between. A mediator. It's very important that he succeed. A good deal more important, frankly, than causing you distress.

(Pause)

MONAGH Yes. I'm living a disposable life.

GIRL You have a career.

MONAGH Aren't I the lucky one.

GIRL May I ask you what you plan to do?

MONAGH Well . . . I rather thought I might try and change the course of Irish history. Assassinate the Queen, maybe. Sit down in the middle of Belfast and set fire to myself. I have to warn you, though, I'm not very good at plans. I'm still making plans for my twenty-first birthday party. And that was eight years ago. *(She tries to smile).* I still haven't decided what to wear.

GIRL I think a letter would be best. I'd prefer you not to visit him again.

MONAGH You do a very classy line in hatred.

GIRL I don't feel any hatred for you. I've wasted very little time thinking about you at all. I've wasted very little time on any of his girlfriends. Only when it's called for. Thank you for talking to me. Good luck with your career.

She goes. As the light fades on MONAGH, *we hear the recording of her singing:*

> But oh my, I was the lucky one,
> They all wanted to be by my side
> While you were left as the lonely one
> Out in the shadows it's easy to hide,
> But nobody knows how I'm crying inside
> Because it was you that he chose for his bride
> You know it's funny but true
> Aren't you the lucky one too
> Aren't you the lucky one too
> Aren't you the lucky one too.

During this, lights come up on:

> MARTYN *at the door holding an open letter.* ROY *standing at the piano. They stare at one another in silence.*

MARTYN What should we do?
ROY Ignore it.
MARTYN We'd better clear out.
ROY Burn it, we're not going through that again.
MARTYN We'd be okay in London.
ROY We're starting to happen here. We can't just jettison that because of some twisted screwball.
MARTYN *(looking at the envelope)* It's got a Belfast postmark.

> ROY *sits down at the piano and plays a few jagged chords.*

It was posted only the day before yesterday.
ROY Will you stop drivelling on about it!
MARTYN I'm trying to keep my lunch down.

> ROY *gets up, takes the letter, looks at it, gives it back, sits down again.*

MARTYN You're always talking about London
ROY Ultimately. When we're ready for it. When we've got an established reputation as a hit-making team.
(They cast around silently).
MARTYN We could take it to the police.
ROY Waste of time.
MARTYN The typing might give them some kind of lead. *(He looks at the letter).*
ROY So what? What could they do about it?
MARTYN *(reading it out in a menacing accent)* 'Just so you know till expect a visit one of these days. Don't think you're safe hid for you're not. We have got your number'.
ROY It's like some form of leprosy.
MARTYN 'Unclean, Unclean'.
ROY The whole country's a pestilential swamp.
MARTYN Stagnant. Sick. We'd be far better off out of it.
ROY They're not intimidating me out of my own job and home.
MARTYN Home? Home is just a place where you can hide away. As the songwriter puts it.

ROY	I've no reason to hide. *(He plays a defiant phrase or two)*. What have you got?
MARTYN	You're joking.
ROY	Come on, cough it up.
MARTYN	I can't write a song with a death threat in my hand!
ROY	Look, we've got to keep delivering product. *(He notices* MARTYN *listening)*. What is it?
MARTYN	I thought I heard a noise.
	(They both listen. Silence)
ROY	There's nothing.
	(He plays a jaunty fragment of tune).
MARTYN	In one ear and out the other one.
ROY	What is?
MARTYN	It's an idea for that tune. Something like, every time my girl and I go walking, I try to win her love with my sweet talking, but I something might as well not bother, for all my words and sighs and little white lies go in one ear and out the other. Then the hook, *(sings)* In one ear and out the other one, in one ear . . .
ROY	Bit awkward.
MARTYN	It needs the right beat. Disco.

ROY *tries out some half-hearted phrases on the piano.*
MARTYN *continues slowly deliberating out loud.*

	Honey don't spoil my fun. Our conversation's just begun. Put away that big bad gun. But she didn't see what I meant. She pulled that trigger and the bullet went. *(Sings)*. In one ear and out the other one, in one ear . . .
ROY	Cut that out!
MARTYN	It's a possible bridge.
ROY	It's not funny.
MARTYN	What's eating you?

The door is knocked loudly, off. They pale visibly.

	We're not expecting anybody.
ROY	Maybe it's Monagh.
MARTYN	You said she was up with Playfair for the weekend.
ROY	Maybe it's the postman.
MARTYN	With another letter.
ROY	*(moving)* I'll go.
MARTYN	Don't be mad.
ROY	It's just somebody at the door.

MARTYN   *(calling)* Who is it, please?
         (Silence)
ROY   They didn't hear you.
MARTYN   Look out the window.

> ROY *goes off.*

         Do you recognise them?
ROY   *(off)* I can't see anything.

> MARTYN *goes off. Pause. Sound of the door being opened and closed. They come back.*

MARTYN   Who would it have been?
         (ROY shrugs)
ROY   What'll we do?
MARTYN   Maybe it was somebody canvassing. Or collecting.
         (ROY picks up the letter and scrumples it).
ROY   We'd better get packed for London.

> *Blackout. Music.*

STAGE

> MONAGH *in a follow spot with a hand mike.*

MONAGH   *(sings)* The banks are blowing up throughout the land
                   I'm catching all the pennies in my hand
                   They're falling twice as hard as I can stand
                   The breakdown man is greatly in demand

                   When I was a young girl
                   I climbed the highest trees
                   I crawled out on the rooftops
                   Upon my hands and knees

                   So take me higher daddy
                   Take me higher please
                   Show me how your elevator climbs
                   Don't think you can satisfy me
                   Till you fly me
                   Higher than you did the other times

I always wanted mountains
Hills just wouldn't do
I gotta get above the clouds
Where nothing spoils the view

So take me higher daddy
Take me higher please
Lift me till my head can scrape the sky
I can't stand this world below me
Don't let go me
Show me some escape before I die

I don't want no miner
I need a steeplejack
I want to keep going up
Till there's no going back
So take me higher daddy
Take me higher please
Take me on an escalator ride
Don't you see you just frustrate me
Elevate me
Lately I've been so dissatisfied

Oh, take me higher daddy
Take me higher please
Show me how your rocket-ship can roar
Down here the devils hound me
Crawling all around me
Pounding on my walls and on my door . . .

I need a steeplejack
I need a steeplejack
I need a steeplejack
I need a steeplejack.

Blackout.

A & R OFFICE

The lights come up on the MAN—*as a record company
A & R boss, Spalding—seated behind a desk.* ROY *in
front of it in his overcoat.*

MAN	Where's your partner, Roy?
ROY	He's down with the 'flu.
MAN	Our lovely London weather, eh?
ROY	He's really sorry not to have met you.
MAN	There's interesting potential in some of these demos. How long have you two been writing together?
ROY	Just nine months professionally.
MAN	You'll appreciate that a company like ours needs to be sure of a steady output of good product.
ROY	That's guaranteed, no problem.
MAN	I tell you what we'll do, Roy. Send me in all your product, for the whole nine months, every little thing you've done, the entire catalogue. We'll talk it around in here, and you and your partner pop in again on the thirty-first.
ROY	Fine.
MAN	I'll arrange for you to be paid a small retainer to cover this. No commitment either way, of course. If we should decide to use any of the songs, that'll be treated as a separate matter. How's that?
ROY	Great.
MAN	Lovely. One other thing, Roy, and I must be honest. I should lose the lady if I were you.
ROY	Monagh?
MAN	In cabaret, in the right dress, if you'd had a few gins, maybe. On record, not a hope. Too old, too ordinary, and twopence a dozen.
ROY	We all work together, you see. It's a package.
MAN	You've got a contractual arrangement, have you?
ROY	It's just an understanding.
MAN	I don't see any problem in that case.
ROY	We're friends.
MAN	Suit yourself. It's your career.
	(Slight pause)
ROY	Is there somebody particular you'd like us to write for?
MAN	Let's be quite clear, Roy, that the company isn't at this stage making you any sort of offer. Any offer that might materialise would be contingent on the outcome of these propositions I've laid before you.
ROY	I realise.
MAN	But if we were to get to the actual point of doing business—I'd be asking you to supply material for a couple of young acts. A couple of schoolgirls we've recently signed. Dynamite voices. Lovely little things

too. I think one of them's going to be very big.
(*Pause*)

ROY   That sounds exciting.

MAN   We *were* hoping to break them over the summer. But to be perfectly honest, Roy, we don't have the songs yet. It's a tough end of the market, solo females is, well, you know yourself.

ROY   I think there's a change due though . . .

MAN   Talk it over, see what you come up with, Roy, give me a little tinkle in three weeks, all right?

Blackout.

ROY AND MARTYN'S FLAT

MARTYN *sitting in pyjamas and dressing gown holding a telegram with one hand, pouring a glass of orange juice and vodka with the other, chuckling to himself.* ROY *enters, throwing off his coat.*

ROY   It's not good.

MARTYN   (*holding up his glass*) I give you Fletcher and Semple . . .

ROY   They don't want Monagh.

MARTYN   . . . who have just been chosen, my friend . . . to represent Ireland . . . at the Ettelbruck Song Contest.
(ROY *stares in silent disbelief*)

ROY   Says who?

MARTYN   (*holding up telegram*) Dublin.

ROY   What with?

MARTYN   'Crybaby'.

ROY   Where is it?

MARTYN   Luxembourg.

ROY   When?

MARTYN   Twenty-seventh to thirty-first of this month.
(ROY *takes the telegram, peruses it*).
They're flying us over. All expenses paid.

ROY   My knees are shaking.

MARTYN   Have some of this.

ROY   I thought you'd the 'flu.

MARTYN   I've begun to recover.
(ROY *drinks*).

ROY   I've never heard of it, have you?

MARTYN	It's in Luxembourg. We can go to Paris. The Louvre. The Rive Gauche.
ROY	I wonder if it carries any weight.
MARTYN	It's a free holiday.
ROY	This is serious!
MARTYN	'Crybaby'? You call that serious?
ROY	It's a bright catchy song.
MARTYN	*(sings mockingly)* 'Don't be a crybaby, if you wanna be my baby . . .'
ROY	It's a Europe kind of song, that's why they chose it. If she could win this thing, it might change his mind.
MARTYN	Whose mind?
ROY	Spalding. The A & R chief.
MARTYN	I forgot all about that, what did he say?
ROY	He liked the songs.
MARTYN	You mentioned something about Monagh.
ROY	He wants us to get rid of her. *(Pause)*
MARTYN	What did *you* say?
ROY	No dice. I told him we're a team. It's a package deal. Take it or leave it. *(Pause)*
MARTYN	What was he offering?
ROY	Nothing—yet. He wanted us to show him everything we'd written, the whole collection. Then he'd let us know at the end of the month.
MARTYN	*(rising)* I'll get it all together.
ROY	What's the point?
MARTYN	It's the third biggest record company in England, that's the point. It's arriving at long last, a guaranteed salary. Prestige. A civilised life-style. Instead of this.
ROY	We're not breaking up the team.
MARTYN	There is no godforsaken team! We're in London, she's in Dublin.
ROY	Once we get fixed up . . .
MARTYN	She doesn't care. She's stopped even trying. She's not concerned.
ROY	We're starting to happen. This song contest's a real chance to prove it.
MARTYN	A chance to finish it, you mean. Amicably. We've got her on the air, got her into records, and now she has the chance to see Ettelbruck and die. A fitting conclusion to a fabulous partnership. No regrets, still the best of friends, you can even marry her if you like.

ROY This has nothing to do with my personal feelings, Martyn, I want you to realise that.

MARTYN It's the biggest chance we're ever going to get, Roy.

Blackout. The band plays the tune of 'Crybaby'.

PUB

Soft lights come up on the GIRL—*as Meryl Shanks, a journalist—sitting on a bar stool taking notes, with* ROY *and* MARTYN *on either side of her holding drinks,* MARTYN *laughing.*

MARTYN Stripped stark bare! Not a stitch! Caught red-handed wasn't the half of it. And Roy and me clutching big beakers of bubbly.

ROY If it hadn't happened, we might still be teaching.

MARTYN But the gem of it is, he takes a long look at Monagh—that's the girl—draws himself up, and says, 'Never in my career have I encountered such bare-faced effrontery'. *(He laughs. Pause).*

GIRL Marvellous.

MARTYN So then we started writing songs full-time.

GIRL In Belfast?

ROY Right.

GIRL You mean there's an actual music scene there—as such?

MARTYN Oh yeah. There's a couple of first-rate studios.

GIRL What about—you know—clubs and things?

MARTYN There's a certain number of clubs, yeah.

GIRL Ooh. One rather forms the impression here in London that they've all been blown up long since.

MARTYN No, not at all. There's a certain amount of terrorist involvement in show business, of course.

GIRL Ooh. Really.

MARTYN You know, illegal clubs, racketeering, intimidation. All that stuff.

GIRL Did you experience any of that?

MARTYN Not a lot, apart from two death threats.
(Uneasy pause. ROY *exchanges a look with* MARTYN*).*
It happens to a lot of people. Social workers. Journalists. Anybody. Rumours and smear stories.

ROY We really got properly started in the business in Dublin.

GIRL	Is that why you moved to Dublin?
ROY	What?
GIRL	The threats?
MARTYN	The thing of it is, Meryl . . . we need to be a bit careful.
ROY	We'd rather not go into it.
GIRL	Fine.
	(Slight pause)
ROY	Actually, the others'll be arriving soon, we'd better get back to the flat.
GIRL	Ooh. Yes. *(She starts off)*.
MARTYN	*(as he follows)* The Fletcher and Semple Story, End of Part One!

Blackout. The band plays 'Crybaby' bright and fast. Stops abruptly.

Roy and Martyn's Flat

A burst of laughter: lights up on a party scene. The GIRL *and the* WOMAN—*as Meryl Shanks and Mrs. Smiley, a music industry publicist from Dublin—are seated on the sofa.* ROY, MARTYN *and the* MAN—*as Spalding—are standing. All have drinks. Their laughter peters out.* MONAGH *is speaking from beside a drinks trolley.*

MONAGH	So then they moved in on a big fat close-up. You know, the pitted pores and the mouth grazing the microphone and the big cow eyes mooning straight into the camera. At which point a fleck of spittle appeared on his fat lip. A large globule of white slime, squatting right there in full view, looming closer and closer. Whereupon . . . the middle finger of his hand entered the picture . . . all hairy, and knobbly with rings . . . and he flicked the spittle away. I nearly spewed all over the set.
MAN	He's an artiste who's worked a long time to get to the top.
WOMAN	His voice is adorable, isn't it.
MAN	His first album went gold a few months back.
WOMAN	It's so warm and soothing.
	(Pause).
MAN	*(to* MONAGH*)* You get the same programmes as we do, then?

MONAGH	Pardon?
MAN	In Northern Ireland . . . you get our television programmes, do you?
MONAGH	Now and then—if the wind's in the right quarter.
	(ROY appears with a bottle).
ROY	Another drink, Mrs. Smiley?
WOMAN	I will in a minute, lovie.
ROY	Mr. Spalding?
MONAGH	Why don't we all just help ourselves when the need arises?
	(She liberally does do).
ROY	Certainly. Everybody feel free.
WOMAN	Do you know, I haven't set foot in Belfast for eight or nine years, it must be.
MAN	During the war was my only time there.
GIRL	*(to MONAGH)* It's amazingly brave of you to live there.
MONAGH	Never give it a second thought, do we, lads? Dodging your way through a hail of bullets to fight for the last loaf of bread in the shop . . . it comes naturally to us.
GIRL	Really, though—it's very hard for us to imagine what it must be like.
MONAGH	I'll tell you what it's like . . .
ROY	We all live in Dublin now, you see.
MONAGH	You know these items you see in the papers every so often. The latest world record for staying underground buried alive in a coffin. I don't know whether you've noticed . . . but the cretin who does it is always an Irishman. Comes naturally to us. Breathing through a straw, crapping into your absorbent underpants. That's what it's like.
	(Slight pause).
WOMAN	I think you must be a Scorpio, Monagh.
MONAGH	Cancer. Lovie.
MARTYN	Are you keen on astrology, Mrs. Smiley?
WOMAN	Oh, I follow my horoscope religiously, isn't it terrible?
MONAGH	With the moon lodged in the lower bicuspid.
ROY	I hope ours were favourable for the week ahead anyway —for the Song Contest.
MONAGH	I've read them. I read all the papers in the plane coming to London. They all said the same thing. On no account go anywhere . . . this week . . . because there's nowhere left worth the trip. Not even the moon. Especially not the moon. Why don't you two ever write a song about the good old moon?

MARTYN   I could never think of a good rhyme for it.
MONAGH   *(singing)* By the light of the silvery *moon* . . . I love to
          spoon . . . with my honey I'll *croon* . . . love's *tune* . . .
ROY   Okay, Monagh . . .
MONAGH   . . . Honey*moon* . . . keep a-shining in *June* . . . your
          silvery beams will light love's dreams, we'll be cuddling
          soon . . . by the light of the *moon*.
MARTYN   Yeah, that pretty well cornered the market.
MONAGH   I wish to God they'd never gone near it. It's polluted
          now. Everybody was so excited, I wasn't excited, I cried
          my piggy little eyes out. It was just a dirty beach. One
          of them even said that . . . just a dirty beach they'd
          brought with them in their heads. It gives all the songs
          a new twist, doesn't it? *(Sings)*. Somewhere there's
          music, how high the moon . . . *(speaks)* high as a
          wrestler's jockstrap.
          (Uncomfortable silence as she pours herself a drink).
MAN   I shall have to be off, I'm afraid.
WOMAN   *(rising also)* Would you ever be able to drop me at
          my hotel, Mr. Spalding? It's not very far.
MAN   Certainly, a pleasure.
ROY   We'll be seeing you in the morning, then, Mrs. Smiley?
WOMAN   Aren't they adorable fellas, these two rascals?
MAN   I like their spirit, I must say.
MARTYN   Thanks for dropping in, Mr. Spalding.
MAN   My pleasure, Martyn, nice to meet you. Give me a little
          tinkle when you get back from the Continent and I'll
          let you know what's what. All right?
MARTYN   The minute we're back.
MAN   Nice to meet you all.
WOMAN   Yes, indeed. Cheerio, lovies.
GIRL   Bye.

ROY *and* MARTYN *escort the* MAN *and* WOMAN *off.*

MONAGH   What kind of a name is Meryl?
GIRL   Ooh. Well. My eldest sister was given Beryl, then the
          second one was Cheryl, so I suppose I just had to be
          Meryl.
MONAGH   Any brothers?
GIRL   Not actually, no.
MONAGH   That's a blessing. *(She pours a drink)*. Mrs. Smiley is a
          publican for the Irish music industry.
GIRL   Yes. Quite. A publicist, you mean.

MONAGH	No, I mean a publican. She sustains the flow of drink at a constant level. It's her one redeeming feature.
GIRL	She didn't actually clue me in—fully, I mean—on just what was happening.
MONAGH	God himself would be hard put. What rag do you write for?
GIRL	I'm a free-lance.
MONAGH	When you think about it, we've had quite a Biblical crowd here tonight. A scribe. A pharisee. A publican. Jesus Christ. And God the Father Almighty. I gather it's the entry into Jerusalem.
GIRL	And which part do you play?
MONAGH	I'm the shagging donkey.
GIRL	Yes, I gather that the Spalding man is probably going to offer a contract to your friends?
MONAGH	We gather alike.
GIRL	They were telling me a perfectly amazing story about receiving death threats.
MONAGH	Were they now? So you've been getting the whole thrilling saga of their turbulent rise to fame?
GIRL	How exactly did it come about?
MONAGH	It's not unusual. It happens every day. Innocent people. Some of them get more than threats. Some of them get shot. Some of them even go and bloody die. *(She grabs the whiskey bottle, sees that it's empty and tosses it away).* It's Hunt the Booze Time. The private supply. Bet you I know where they've got it.

She wanders off.

GIRL	It was just random threats, then, was it?

She follows MONAGH *off. Stage empty for a moment. Sound of final farewells and door being closed from off.*

ROY	*(entering)* Where is she?
MARTYN	*(entering)* Where's Meryl?
	*(*ROY *sinks down on the sofa).*
ROY	What the bloody hell is she trying to do to me?
MARTYN	I never dreamed she'd take it this hard.
ROY	Her whole behaviour was just an attempt at sabotage.
MARTYN	She's had it, Roy.
ROY	She's ruined her chances with Spalding, that's for sure.
MARTYN	She damned near ruined ours.
ROY	They must be in the kitchen.

MARTYN   *(picks up empty bottle)* She got through practically all of this single-handed. That's what she'll be after.

> The GIRL *appears in the doorway.*

ROY   God only knows what she's telling that bird-brained reporter.

MARTYN   Hello there, Meryl.

GIRL   I'm afraid that girl, your friend, seems rather distraught.

MARTYN   Is she in the kitchen?

GIRL   We were just talking, and then she literally ran off into the night. Into that sort of waste ground at the back.

ROY   We'd better go after her.

GIRL   Would it seem awful of me to slip off? I'm rather late for another appointment . . .

ROY   That's okay.

MARTYN   We're sorry for what was inflicted on you.

GIRL   Ooh. I loved every minute. Really did. I'm sure I can place a piece about you both.

MARTYN   That's terrific, Meryl.

GIRL   Perhaps we can talk again sometime.

MARTYN   Certainly. Anytime.

GIRL   Well, bye.
          (She exits. MARTYN *follows).*

MARTYN   *(off)* Safe home.

ROY   *(from door)* Cheers.

> MARTYN *re-enters.*

ROY   We'd better get some torches.

> *Blackout. The band plays 'Crybaby'.*

PARKING LOT

> *The beams of two torches flicker across the dark stage.* ROY *and* MARTYN *are heard calling Monagh's name from off. They enter, flashing the torches into the corners of the stage; one of them picks out* MONAGH, *huddled on the ground, staring straight ahead. They train both torches on her.*

ROY	Are you all right? What's wrong?
MONAGH	*(voice dead)* He was filming. There was shooting. It was in the paper.
MARTYN	She's raving.
ROY	No, it's Playfair. Something's happened. Monagh. It's Playfair, isn't it.
MONAGH	He was hit. They shot him. He's dead. *(Pause).*
ROY	Help her up.

They hoist her to her feet and help her off in silence. The torchlight flickers disappear.

STADIUM

Flood of light. The band plays a fanfare. The WOMAN *sweeps on in a gaudy full-length dress, carrying a mike, grinning hugely.*

WOMAN   An elo, dir Dammen en dir Hären, ass de Moment komm, wo deï distinguëert Dammen en Hären vun onsem Jury hîrt Schlussurteel ofzegin hun. Mir werden also elo geschwenn wessen, wien de Gewenner vun desem allereïschten Ettelbrecker Internationalen Gesangsfestival ass. Dir sit bestemmt eens mat mir, wann ech soen, dass net nemmen eent, mais vill vun deenen Lidder, deï mir bejëert hun, de Preis verdengen. Eise Jury huet et bestemmt net lîcht. Wahrend de Jury nun sein Endresultat vîrbereet, wöllt de Willi Zero ons nach e besschen ennerhâlen, an zwar sengt hien ons dat Lidd: the Zig Zag Song!

She goes off, as the MAN, *loudly dressed as Willy Zero, runs on with a hand mike. The band strikes up. As he sings, he tacks back and forth across the stage, swerving his knees from side to side.*

MAN   *(sings)*   Sing hello the Zig Zag song
Sing bye-bye the Zig Zag song
It's a song that all can sing
Come along and let it ring

Sing it low the Zig Zag song
Sing it high the Zig Zag song
Do the Zig Zag as you go
Now the chorus goes just so:

La-la-la-la-la-la-la
La-la-la-la-la-la-la
La-la-la-la-la-la-la
La-la-la-la-la-la-la

Zigging Zagging up and down
Zigging Zagging round the town
Oh, la-la-la-la-la-la-la
La-la-la-la-la-la-la

Now you know the Zig Zag song
All join in the Zig Zag song
To and fro the Zig Zag song
All begin the Zig Zag song

Sing it low — Zig Zag song
Sing it high — Zig Zag song
Do the Zig Zag as you go
Now the chorus goes just so:

La-la-la-la-la-la-la
La-la-la-la-la-la-la
La-la-la-la-la-la-la
La-la-la-la-la-la-la

And that's how you do the Zig Zag song!

*He zig zags off and the lights fade out. The band plays
on in double time in the darkness.*

AIRPORT LOUNGE

*Bright harsh fluorescent glare. A row of moulded plastic
seats.* ROY *on the end one reading a newspaper.* MARTYN
*behind him. Both dressed in very flashy showbiz formal
wear—ruffled shirt-fronts, floppy bow ties, hugh cuff-
links—but all of it ravaged by several days without*

sleep. They talk and move like sleep-walkers. MONAGH *is further down the row, sprawled out, her head lolling on her chest.*

MARTYN   It's all there. Everything. *(Reading).* 'Terrorist Girl Who Calls The Tune'.

ROY   Christ!

MARTYN   *(reading)* 'Songwriters Roy Fletcher and Martyn Semple . . . a somewhat unusual start to their careers . . . traditional-style Republican martyr-ballads—on commission . . . "We don't talk much about it these days", says Martyn, 29, wryly . . .'

ROY   She must have pumped Monagh for it. Evil bitch.

MARTYN   Wait till Marie Kyle sees it.

ROY   *(thrusting paper aside)* Ah, to hell. What's the time?

MARTYN   *(looking at his watch)* Just after seven.

ROY   A.m. or p.m.?

MARTYN   I don't know. *(More frightened)* I don't know. What was it like coming in?

ROY   Twilight.

MARTYN   Either way. There's no windows.

ROY   Maybe there's a strike or something.

MARTYN   They won't let her on the plane like that, Roy.
(ROY moves down and slaps MONAGh on the cheeks).

ROY   Monagh. Pull out of it. We have to get on the plane now. Monagh.
(She moans a little but doesn't move).
Her handbag's full of pills.

MARTYN   Not as full as she is.
(ROY returns and sits again).

MARTYN   We're not in the right place, Roy.

ROY   The airport. It's the airport. There's only one.

MARTYN   Where's the plane, then?

ROY   It doesn't go till ten.

MARTYN   P.m. or a.m.? *(Pause).* We're early.

ROY   The money's spent. I don't even feel tired any more.

MARTYN   I feel corroded. My flesh. I wish they'd turn the lights off.

ROY   That Swiss song was gunk.

MARTYN   What was it about, anyway?

ROY   How do I know? Cuckoo clocks.

MARTYN   You could tell it would win. It was the elbow routine. The crowd fell for that.

ROY   We should have walked it.

MARTYN	After her shoe came off—I couldn't watch any more.
ROY	She mixed up the chorus and the verse. It was just like gibberish. The band didn't know what to do. They limped on behind her but she was all out of key. You couldn't describe it as singing at all. It was just a prolonged howl. I had to go and help her off at the end. *(Pause)*.
MARTYN	Hey, we never opened our telegrams. *(He takes four greetings telegrams and a larger packet from his case . . . He opens the first one, glances at it)*. I think we ought to change our style, you know. Get back to the roots. *(Reads):* 'Monagh my sweet may your Crybaby cry all the way to the bank. Cyril.' *(He tosses the telegram back in the case)*.
ROY	What roots?
MARTYN	Something ethnic. The heritage of the past. *(He opens another telegram, glances at it)*.
ROY	Cecilia Street Primary School. Rock 'n' roll. Football. The pictures. That's my roots.
MARTYN	I mean further back than that. The country's history. The old culture. The tradition. *(Throws telegram into case)*.
ROY	That's got nothing to do with me. It's got nothing to do with you either.
MARTYN	I'd an uncle who was a fluent Irish speaker. I was pretty good at it at school too.
ROY	You're no more a Gaelic speaker than I am.
MARTYN	You? You've never learnt a word of it.
ROY	I picked up a few phrases once from a tourist brochure. It was in a Chinese restaurant in Cork.
MARTYN	*(opening another telegram)* Extraordinary people, the Chinese. I've been reading them up, you know. I've been thinking them over.
ROY	They write lousy tunes.
MARTYN	A quarter of the world's people. And nobody owns anything. It's all held in common. They all work for each other. For the common good. *(Throws telegram in case)*.
ROY	The Japanese are a different story, however.
MARTYN	The only thing that bothers me is—I've yet to hear of a Chinese joke. I don't mean Chinese laundry jokes—chop-chop flied lice all that stuff—I mean one of their own. A Red Chinese gag. They don't appear to have a sense of humour. The way we do. It's a serious draw-

back, that, in my opinion. It could very well end up endangering world peace.
(He opens another telegram).
Of course I might be mistaken. I might have it wrong. The way they see things—maybe *we're* a Chinese joke. *(He throws the telegram into the case).*

ROY   You don't even like folk songs.

MARTYN   Some. Not all.

ROY   I hate them.

MARTYN   This'll ruin us, Roy. We'll be blacklisted.

ROY   They won't blame us. The song was all right. It's the end of the line for her, though.

MARTYN   Maybe we should get her to a doctor.

ROY   She'll be all right. It'll pass off. Anyway, all the money's spent.

MARTYN   We've got a present.
(He begins to pick at the tape on the remaining package).

MARTYN   I feel as if we've been here for days already. Years. Maybe the whole airport's been hijacked. Maybe all the ground staff are pinned down in their offices. By terrorist guns. The control tower paralysed. All the planes flying round and round stacked up above us. Running out of fuel. Any minute now they'll start falling out of the sky like asphyxiated flies. *(Pause).* It hasn't turned out the way we thought it would, Roy.

ROY   Not much.

MARTYN   It's not the way we dreamed it would be.

ROY   Not yet.

MARTYN   How long are we going to have to wait in this place?

He rips the tape off the package. Simultaneously—Blackout. Explosion. A noisy drum intro. The band strikes up. A red spot comes on. Showing MONAGH *on her feet, smiling brightly, with a hand mike.* ROY *and* MARTYN'S *seats are toppled over. In the red glow, we see them on their knees, hands and faces covered in blood, groping about blindly.*

MONAGH   *(sings)* Laugh and the world laughs with you,
                Cry and you cry alone,
                If you plan to make me love you,
                If you want me for your own —

Don't be a crybaby
If you wanna be my baby
For when you're smiling
You're the apple of my eye
Don't heave a sigh baby
There's no earthly reason why baby
You know that loving is something
Money can't buy
You know that loving is really something
Money can't buy!

Blackout. END.